# Finding Out About
# TUDOR
# AND STUART
# TOWNS

# Madeline Jones

Batsford Academic and Educational Ltd *London* A450

# —Contents—

Typeset by Tek-Art Ltd London SE20
and printed in Great Britain by
R.J. Acford Ltd
Chichester, Sussex
for the publishers
Batsford Academic and Educational Ltd,
an imprint of B T Batsford Ltd,
4 Fitzhardinge Street
London W1H 0AH

ISBN 0 7134 4293 X

## ACKNOWLEDGMENTS

The author and publishers would like to
thank the following for their kind permission
to reproduce copyright illustrations: Bromley
Library, pages 20, 22; Glamorgan Archive
Service, page 7; Pat Hodgson Library, page 21
(right); Kent Archives Office, page 34 (and
also for the extracts from *Kentish Sources:*
*Crime and Punishment*, page 35); A.F. Kersting,
page 16; Oxford University, Ashmolean
Museum, Department of Western Art, pages
18-19; University of London Library, page 19
(top). The picture on page 6 comes from
William Dugdale, *The Antiquities of Warwick-
shire* (1656). The map on page 47 was drawn
by Rudolph Britto.

# Introduction

The Tudor period in English history began in 1485, and the Stuart period ended in 1714. Over two hundred years is a long time, and though life changed more slowly then than it does today, the towns were not quite the same in 1714 as they had been in 1485. You will notice some of the changes as you read through this book. You will notice too the many ways in which Tudor and Stuart town life was different from our life today — and perhaps some ways in which it was almost the same.

One big difference was that far fewer people lived in towns, only about one in every ten at the start of the period and about one in four or five at the end. We can't be definite about the figures, because no accurate count of the population was made. We know that there were about 700 towns in England and Wales (Scotland and Ireland would need books of their own, so we are not including their towns). Many towns were very small, with only 200 or so houses. Try counting up to 200 houses in your own area today to get some idea of the size.

London was by far the largest town, and as you will see later in the book, it grew during this time. Some other towns also grew, but others got smaller. Daniel Defoe, who wrote about his travels in England just after the end of the Stuart period, was struck by the way that a town's prosperity (and therefore its size) could change:

The fate of things gives a new face to things . . . raises and sinks towns, removes manufactures, and trades; great towns decay, and small towns rise; new towns, new palaces . . . are built every day; great rivers and good harbours dry up, and grow useless; again, new ports are open'd, brooks are made rivers, small rivers navigable, ports and harbours are made where none were before, and the like.

You may be able to find out whether your local town was doing well or badly at this time, and why.

Even in a small town, townsmen felt special. They often looked down on country people. Towns had many privileges, and ran their own affairs. Large towns had a Mayor or Lord Mayor and a local Council, led by a group of Aldermen. The Council made rules for the town, raised money and kept order. Below the Councillors came the Freemen, who had the right to buy and sell goods and to set up workshops in the town. They were often the people with the right to vote too, in elections for Mayors or MPs. Although the number of freemen varied from town to town, it never

Towns were small, and it was easy to walk out into the country.

3

included more than about half the men (and women did not have the right to be free-women).

Every town had some inhabitants who were very poor. Townsmen learnt that these people must be looked after; otherwise they would become desperate and start rioting. If a riot did take place, the rich townsmen's houses were attacked and their expensive glass windows were broken. It was good sense, as well as a good deed, to see that the poor did not go hungry. The custom of collecting a "poor rate" to provide funds to help the poor first began in the towns of Tudor England. Some towns even set up workshops for the unemployed.

There is a lot of interesting material, both written and visual, to tell us what Tudor and Stuart towns were like. This book will give you some samples: you will, if you are interested, be able to find more for yourselves. You will also be able to find more topics to study. In a short book like this one, we can only start you off on the search.

Here are some suggestions about tracking down information.

### 1 PEOPLE TO ASK
*Librarians* The Librarian in the Reference Section (or the Local History section if there is one) of your Public Library will be able to tell you if there are any old or modern histories of the town. She or he will probably also know where to find any Tudor or Stuart documents still available.

### 2 VISUAL MATERIAL
a) *Walking round the town* Look for Tudor or Stuart houses or public buildings like a Town Hall. Study the street names. Look for Tudor or Stuart tombs in churches or cathedrals. You may be able to get a "Town Trail" leaflet from the Library to help you.

b) *Maps and pictures* Try the Library, too, for old views of the town, and old maps. The Town Hall may have portraits of Tudor or Stuart townsmen.

c) *Objects* Local museums often have old furniture, cooking utensils, etc. There may be some plate (silver objects) in the Town Hall, dating from Tudor or Stuart times: ask the Town Clerk for permission for a group visit to see the town's treasures.

### 3 WRITTEN SOURCES
First, some special problems with Tudor and Stuart documents:

(i) *Handwriting* — this is difficult to read. It can be done if you are keen, but needs a lot of practice. Start on photostat copies which you can puzzle out at home. Usually, the later the date of the document the easier it is to read.

(ii) *Spelling* — this varies greatly as spelling

was not yet fixed. If a word looks strange try saying it aloud. Check the modern spelling of a word in a dictionary if you want to use it in your own writing.

(iii) *Punctuation* — sometimes very few commas or even full stops are used and this can make the meaning hard to make out.

Luckily, there are modern printed versions of many town records. We have taken some extracts from these; in other extracts, you will find the old spelling used. Some old words have been translated into modern English to make a passage easier for you to read — like "victuals (food)" — with the modern version in a bracket after the old version.

a) *Town records* Towns kept written records so that they could look things up: these include records of council meetings and decisions, cases in local law-courts, account-books, lists of freemen and apprentices. Many town records are now in the *County Archives* (in the record-office of the county-town). Your teacher may be able to arrange a visit to see a display: the person to write to is the County Archivist. It is also possible to buy photostat copies of documents from your County Archives.

b) *Inventories and wills* Inventories list the property of people who have died, and wills often name objects, furniture, etc. Both are very useful. There are printed examples in libraries and hand-written inventories in most County Archives.

c) *Local histories and travel books* Your Library may have a town or (more likely) county history written in, or just after, this period. They are very likely to have, or be able to order, the travel books of Celia Fiennes and Daniel Defoe — who may describe your town.

d) *Letters and diaries* You may find local examples of these: diary-writing became fashionable in the seventeenth century. Look in your Library for the diaries of Samuel Pepys and John Evelyn. They lived in or near London, but visited and described many other towns.

*We still read John Stow's "Survey of London" to find out about Tudor London. His monument is in the church of St Andrew Undershaft, Leadenhall Street, London.*

# Looking at the Town

A traveller approaching a Tudor or Stuart town would often first see a church spire or tower — the highest building in the town. Often, too, he would come up to high town walls, and enter the town through a stone gateway. Towns no longer protected themselves with new walls, as there was less danger of fighting than in the past, but many had walls already. One new set of walls — at Berwick-on-Tweed — *was* built in Tudor times. Find Berwick on a map, and perhaps you can suggest a reason for this (ask yourself what neighbours might attack it).

## WORCESTER IN 1698

A Stuart lady, Celia Fiennes, travelled through the country on horse-back. It is interesting to see what she picked out to describe when visiting a town:

'Worcester town . . . is washed by the river Severn, its a large Citty, 12 Churches, the streetes most of them broad, the buildings some of them are very good and lofty, its encompass'd (surrounded) with a wall which has 4 gates that are very strong; the Market place is large; there is a Guildhall (Town Hall) besides the Markethouse which stands on pillars of stone; the Cathedral stands in a large yard . . . its a lofty magnificent building . . . .

Celia Fiennes was quite rich, and used to living in London, so she was not easily impressed. What do you think would most impress an ordinary villager who came in from the country to a town like Worcester, or Coventry (shown in the picture)? What would you think worth describing in a town you visited today?

A view of early Stuart Coventry. In the Civil War, the townsmen shut the gates to keep out Charles I's army. In 1662, Charles II had the walls pulled down.
▼

This map shows Cardiff in 1610. How many gates are ▶ there? What evidence can you find that Cardiff was growing beyond its old walls?

The Prospect of
COVENTRE
from Warwick roade, on the
south side of the Cittye

You can see from the map of Cardiff what a town was like inside its walls. Notice that people making and selling the same goods lived in the same area. (What street names tell you this?) During this period more shops were being set up, where goods were on sale every day, not just on stalls on market days. In Cardiff the butchers at first had stalls under the Town Hall (the "Towne House" on the map). By about 1670 part of the space under the Hall had been made into shops. John Stow tells us how rows of shops came into being in Tudor London:

> . . . these houses, now possessed by fish-mongers, were at first but moveable boards (or stalls), set out on market-days, to show their fish there to be sold; but procuring license to set up sheds, they

grew to shops, and by little and little to tall houses of three or four stories in height, and now are called Fish Street . . .

Streets were not numbered, and both houses and shops had signs. Numbers only began to be used in some London streets at the very end of the period. If you lived in a town your address would be something like this one (belonging to a London shopkeeper):

> William Browne, at the sign of the Fish, in the lower end of Black Horse Alley, at the steps near Fleet Bridge.

Could you turn your present-day address into one like that — without a house-number or postcode?

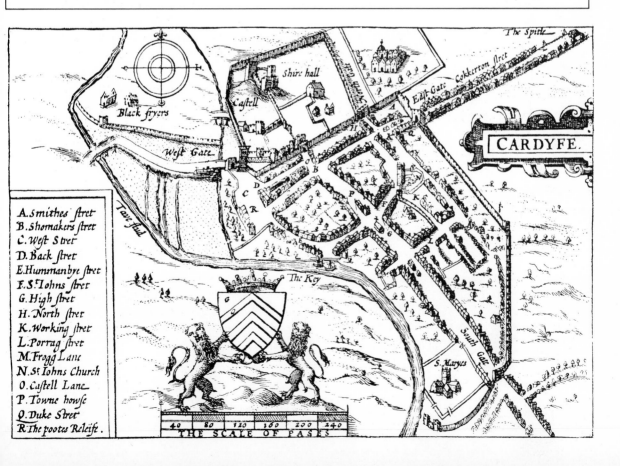

A. Smithes ſtret
B. Shomakers ſtret
C. Weſt S tret
D. Back ſtret
E. Hummanbre ſtret
F. S.ͭ Iohns ſtret
G. High ſtret
H. North ſtret
K. Working ſtret
L. Porrag ſtret
M. Frogg Lane
N. S.ͭ Iohns Church
O. Caſtell Lane
P. Towne howſe
Q. Duke Stret
R. The pootes Releiſe.

THE SCALE OF PASES

# Merchants

The richest townsmen were the merchants, who bought and sold goods in large quantities and often traded overseas. When Celia Fiennes wanted to describe the best houses in a town, she always called them "fit for merchants". London merchants were richest of all, especially those who belonged to big guilds or companies like the Merchant Taylors or, in Stuart times, the East India Company. In small towns, where all the merchants belonged to one guild, their "Guildhall" was used for all town government. That is why some towns still call their Town Hall the "Guildhall".

## BECOMING A MERCHANT

There were regulations to prevent just any ordinary boy from training as an apprentice to a merchant:

> . . . It shall not be lawful to any person dwelling in such market town exercising the art of a merchant trafficking into the parts beyond the seas . . . to take any apprentice . . . except such . . . shall be his son, or else that the father or mother of such apprentice shall have lands . . . of the clear yearly value of £3.
> (Act of Parliament, 1563)

## THE CAREER OF JOHN WHITSON

John Aubrey described the career of John Whitson of Bristol, who died in 1629.

> He was bound apprentice to Alderman Vawr, a Spanish merchant (one who traded with Spain) of this city. He was a handsome young fellow; and his old master the alderman being dead, his mistress . . . after married him . . . . He had a good natural wit (intelligence), and gained by the Spanish trade a fair estate. His second wife was the daughter of Hine, alderman of London, a very beautiful dame as by her picture at length (full-length) in the dining-room doth appear. By her he had a daughter, his only child, who was counted the flower of Bristol, who was married to Sir Thomas Trenchard of Dorsetshire . . .
>
> He lived nobly; kept a plentiful table, and was the most popular magistrate in the city, always chosen a member of Parliament. He kept a noble house, and did entertain and treat the peers and great persons that came to the city. He kept his hawks . . .
>
> He was the greatest benefactor to the city that has been since the Reformation. He gave £500 at least to the City, to maintain blue-coats, boys and maids (to educate poor children). He had a fair house in St. Nicholas Street, where is the stateliest dining roome in the city. He hath been thrice (three times) mayor of this city . . .

You can see here how a man and his family could go up in the world through marriage: why do you think a landowner like Sir Thomas Trenchard was ready to marry a merchant's daughter? Can you spot the ways in which John Whitson spent his money on an impressive life-style?

## GENEROUS MERCHANTS

Like John Whitson, merchants often gave money to their towns. Sometimes they built things and then their names lived on after their deaths. John Stow describes the gift of one London cloth-merchant:

William Lambe, gentleman and cloth-worker, in the year 1577, built a water-conduit at Oldborne (Holborn) Cross to his charges of fifteen hundred pounds . . .

*We can tell what wealthy townspeople looked like from tombs like this one in Southwark Cathedral. Alderman Richard Humble, who died in 1616, is shown with his two wives.*

If you look at a street-map of the area of London called Holborn, you can still find "Lamb's Conduit Street".

# Craftsmen

Craftsmen usually worked on the ground floor of their house, and sold their goods from the workshop.

## A ROCHESTER HAT-MAKER

Inventories can help us to find out about craftsmen's houses and shops. William Spilsbey, a hat-maker in Rochester in Kent, had three rooms in his house and a cellar as well as a workshop. When he died in 1703 he left:

**IN THE SHOPP**
four presses two Counters Seaven fine mens hatts fifty three ordinary Hatts for men five fine Hatts for Women seaven old fashioned Hatts for women sixty four Boys and Mens Hatts fourteen fine Boys hatts a parcell of Hatt cases and a box a parcell of Hatt bands ... (worth £24. 14s. in all)

This extract is taken straight from the hand-written inventory, so there is no modern spelling or punctuation. (Where would you put in commas to make it easier to read?) You can find out what "fine Hatts" looked like in 1703 (early in Queen Anne's reign) from a History of Costume. The hats in our picture would have been "old fashioned" by then.

A hatter's workshop. Notice the young apprentice: what is he doing?

## CRAFTSMEN IN LEICESTER

Before setting up shop, a craftsman had to join the right guild or company and also become a freeman of the town. Here is a list of men who became freemen of Leicester in the last three months of 1672. Some were excused a fee because they were the eldest sons of freemen, or paid half the usual fee (that is, 5/- instead of 10/-) because they were a freeman's younger sons. These are marked "s". Those who had been apprentices, and therefore had the right to be freemen if they could pay the full 10/-, are marked "p" (for "prentice"). One (you'll easily pick him out) was an outsider: note the large amount he pays. There were no "freewomen", but the husband of a freeman's eldest daughter had the right to be "free by marriage".

*1672-3*

Oct. 15　John Steeres, p. of George Steeres of Leic., maltster.

Oct. 21　William Bothomley, s. of Jacob Bothomley of Leic., cordwainer (shoemaker), and p. of Thos. Mitchell, late of the Woodgate, baker.

Dec. 4　John Warburton, 2nd s. of Wm. Warburton of Leic., currier (leather-worker) and p. of Wm. Elliott of Leic., ironmonger.

Dec. 9　Henry Ethrington, p. of Thos. Simpson of Leic., tailor.

Dec. 10　Richard Hinckley, p. of Wm. Shewter of Leic., cordwainer.
　　　　Thos. Gilbert, gent, a stranger, £20

**(Register of the Freemen of Leicester.)**

From lists like these you can collect a lot of information about the different crafts in the town. How many can you find in this extract?

## KEEPING OUT "STRANGERS"

During the Stuart period it got more and more difficult to stop people coming into the town and just setting up shop. Town Councils tried to enforce the old rules against non-freemen: in April 1658, the Oxford Chamberlains were ordered to

> **shutt downe the windowes of Thomas Woodward who now keepes a Chandlers Shopp at the upper end of Hollowell, not being a freeman of this Citty, and that they doe from day to day, if the said Woodward shall open them, shutt downe the said windowes.**

Remember that shopfronts at this time usually had wooden shutters, not glass windows — easy enough to "shut down". If Thomas Woodward wanted to go on earning his living in Oxford, what would he have to do?

*A London Shoemaker's sign, 1700.*

11

# Working as an Apprentice

No townsman was supposed to take up a trade or craft unless he had trained as an apprentice, usually for seven years. Girls as well as boys became apprentices, but usually as maid-servants or in crafts like dress-making. An apprentice lived with his or her master and was supposed to be treated like one of the family (this included being beaten for bad behaviour). Sometimes the master was paid to take the apprentice, but often he had to promise to give a small wage as the apprentice grew older, or a suit of clothes at the end of the apprenticeship. The *Bristol Apprentice Rolls* tell us about a girl called Mary Jordan who was bound apprentice in 1626, as a "handmaiden". Her master and mistress promised that after eight years' apprenticeship she should be given

> One gowne and two of petticoats and 2 waistcoates, one for working dayes and thother for Sundayes, two pares of hosen and shoes, 2 aprons, a cople of ruffs and half a dozen of every other sort of linnen apparel.

## LONG HOURS OF WORK

The Sheffield Scissorsmiths made a regulation about working hours in 1680, which shows how hard some apprentices had to work:

> Whereas great mischiefs and inconveniences have heretofore and dailly do arise . . . by some of the said trade or occupation (scissors-making) who . . . do work both themselves, their apprentices and servants most unreasonably . . . whereby many of them become lame and in a little time wholly disenabled (unable) to follow their callings . . . neither we nor any of us,

## AN APPRENTICE IN TUDOR LONDON

Many country gentlemen sent sons as apprentices to London merchants. John Isham of Northamptonshire left school at 16, "at which time it came into his father's mind to place him in London where his other brethren were". In 1542,

> he came up to the aforesayd Cyty and forthwith was bound prentise to one Otwell Hill, . . . of the worshipfull company of the mercers, butt his Master Disceasinge (dying) . . . he (went into) the service of one Thomas Gigges . . . nor disdayninge he at that time any servile woork . . . of caryinge the water . . . bockets to the Thames and such lyke . . . . He thus haveinge run over most happily his dayes of bondage as I may call them . . . he was made free of that notable city of London (he became a freeman) and of the company of the mercers . . .

Notice how the writer praises the young John for doing all kinds of jobs for his masters: many merchants' apprentices thought they were above that kind of thing — can you think why? What interesting fact about Tudor London can we learn from one particular job John was given to do?

> nor any of our apprentices shall . . . during the term of two whole yeares . . . do any manner of work whatsoever belonging to the said trade before the hour of six of the clock in the morning, nor after the hour of eight of the clock in the evening . . .

What strikes you about the Sheffield Scissorsmiths' idea of a reasonable working day?

▲ *This Stuart apprentice is learning to be a calico-printer. He is helping his master to print patterns onto cloth.*

AT the OldKnave of Clubs, at the Bridge-foot in Southwark, Liveth EDWARD BUTLING, who Maketh and Selleth all forts of Hangings for Rooms, in Lengths or in Sheets, Frofted or Plain: Alfo a fort of Paper in Imitation of IrifhStich, of the neweft Fafhion, and feveral other forts, viz. Flock-work, Wainfcot, Marble, Damask, Turkey-Work. Alfo Shop-Books, Pocket-Books, Writing-Paper, Brown-Paper, and Whited-brown Paper, Cards, and all other Sorts of Stationary Wares, Good and Reafonable.

◀ *At the end of the Stuart period, an apprentice could learn the new craft of making wallpaper from a master like Edward Butling.*

# Unruly Apprentices

In spite of their long hours of work, apprentices had time to amuse themselves and to shock their elders by their teenage behaviour.

## RULES FOR NEWCASTLE APPRENTICES

Newcastle merchants were never satisfied with their apprentices. In 1554 they complained that, whereas in the past apprentices had been taught their duty to God and their masters,

> now . . . lewd liberty, instead of the former virtuous life, hath of late taken place in apprentices, and chiefly of those as are serving in this worshipful Fellowship of Merchants . . . (for never among apprentices . . . hath been more abused and inconvenient behaviour than is of them at this day frequented, for what dicing, carding and mumming (taking part in street-plays); what tipling (drinking) dancing and embracing . . . what garded (decorated) coats, jagged hose, lined with silk, and cut shoes, what use of gitters (musical instruments) by night, what wearing of beards, what daggers is by them worn . . .that these their doings are more comely and decent for raging ruffians than seemly for honest apprentices)
> (Book of Orders, Newcastle Merchant Adventurers)

In 1603, rules were made forbidding Newcastle apprentices to:

> weare their haire long nor locks at their eares like ruffians . . . weare any indecent apparell but plain . . . nor to weare any velvet or lace . . . neither any silk garters.

## FIGHTING BETWEEN APPRENTICES

Samuel Pepys describes a battle between rival London apprentices in his Diary for 1664:

> 26th July.
> Great discourse (talk) of the fray yesterday in Moorefields, how the butchers at first did beat the weavers (between whom there hath been ever an old competition for mastery) but at last the weavers rallied and beat them. At first the butchers knocked down all for weavers that had green or blue aprons, till they were fain (obliged) to pull them off and put them in their breeches. At last the butchers were fain to pull off their sleeves, that they might not be known, and were soundly beaten out of the field, and some deeply wounded and bruised; till at last the weavers went out triumphing, calling '£100 for a butcher'.

As you can see, a fight easily got out of hand and people were seriously hurt. Notice the special clothes, belonging to the different trades (many butchers still wear protective sleeves today).

You might like to make up a story about an apprentice. Such stories were popular in Tudor and Stuart times. Generally, the well-behaved apprentice hero ended up rich (like John Isham, or John Whitson on page 8). Lazy and disobedient apprentices came to a bad end.

Rules of 1697 forbade apprentices:

> to get to fencing or dancing schools, nor to music houses, lotteries or playhouses, neither to keep any sort of horses, dogs for hunting or fighting cocks.

*Apprentices were not supposed to go drinking in taverns or ale-houses.*

Remembering the kind of boys who became merchants' apprentices (see page 8), why do you think they were especially hard to keep in order?

# The Poor

Probably about half the population of any town at this time lived on the poverty-line and might need help to keep alive if they became ill or lost their job. Townsmen were prepared to help their own poor, especially the old, the sick and the very young, but they did not feel responsible for outsiders. They worried about the amount they had to pay in poor-rates. Able-bodied people without work were sometimes given work to do at the town's expense. If they seemed unwilling to work, they were whipped as vagrants (this happened to six women as well as to two men in Cardiff in 1576).

*A popular way of helping poor people was to build almshouses, like these in Amersham, Bucks. Each person had his or her own small cottage: notice the separate doors.*

## GENEROUS INDIVIDUALS

You can often find out about gifts made to the poor by reading inscriptions in churches or cathedrals, or sometimes on buildings like the almshouses in the picture. Here is an extract from the will of a Coventry merchant, William Pisford, made in 1517:

> . . . for the term of **10** years, **(I will)** there be dealt about All hallowtide (1st November) twenty furze gowns, and **20** shirts, and smocks, to poor and most needy Men and Women. Also I will that there be dealt every year, for the space of **10** years, in the most coolest of Winter, at divers times, a thousand faggots (bundles of fire-wood) a year . . .

Furze was a heavy, warm material. Why did William Pisford choose early November as the time to make his gift?

## THE POOR IN NOTTINGHAM

The records of Nottingham show the town helping some of the poor:

### Chamberlain's Accounts, 1577-8

| | |
|---|---|
| Item given to 3 maimed soldiers: | 12d |
| Item paid to William Hall for the charges of a poor boy's meat (food) | 4d |
| Item paid to a lame woman at Master Mayor's commandment | 4d |

### 1578-9

| | |
|---|---|
| Item given to Parcar towards his charges to London whereby the town should be no further charged with him | 12d |
| Item given to a blind man | 4d |
| Item given . . . to two poor lame soldiers | 6d |

### Council Minutes, 1615

. . . to set the poor on work . . . there shall be two looms for weaving provided . . .

Nottingham made every effort to keep the number of poor people down, however. (What payment in the Chamberlain's Accounts has already suggested this to us?) In 1612 the Council decided:

> . . . as it is found by daily experience that by the continual building and erecting of new cottages and poor habitations and by the transferring of barns and such like buildings into cottages . . . and likewise by the frequent taking in of inmates into many and poor habitations here, the poorer sort of people do much increase, to the great charge and burden of all the inhabitants of the better sort within this said town . . . from henceforth no . . . freeman of this town shall erect or build any cottage . . . or convert any barn or other building into any cottage . . . without the special license and consent of the Mayor . . . and Aldermen (on pain of a £5 fine).

What do you notice about the attitude of the Councillors to the poor?

## A MISERABLE LIFE FOR LONDON'S POOR

Philip Stubbes wrote an account of the misery of the poor in Tudor London, to shame more people into helping them. Can you think why, in a big city like London, the problem of poverty would be particularly great?

> There is a certayne citie . . . where . . . the poore lye in the streetes, upon pallets of strawe, and well if they have that too, or els in the mire and dirt, as commonly it is seene, having neither house to put in their heades, covering to keepe them from the colde, nor yet to hyde their shame withall, nor a pennie to buy them sustenance, nor any thing else, but are suffered to dye in the streetes like dogges or beastes . . .

# Homes

It is much easier to find out about the homes of the rich townsmen than about those of the poor. Poor people could not afford strong building-materials like brick or stone or even stout timbers. Their one-room shacks have long ago collapsed or been pulled down. They did not own enough furniture for it to be listed after their death in an inventory.

## A PROSPEROUS HOME IN TUDOR LONDON (1592)

This description from a set of stories, called "Cony-catching", about thieves in Tudor London, tells us about a comfortable London house, and the people living there:

> ... his (the visitor's) bed ... was in the same room where they (the family) supped, being commonly called their hall, and there indeed stood a very fair bed, as in such sightly rooms it may easily be thought citizens use not (are not accustomed) to have anything mean or simple.

The mistress . . . suffered all the plate (silver) to stand still on the cupboard, and when she perceived his bed was warmed . . . she and her husband . . . took themselves to their chamber, which was on the same floor, but inward, having another chamber between them and the hall, where the maids and children had their lodging . . . the apprentices, having brought up the keys of the street door, and left them in their master's chamber as they were wont to do, after they had said prayers, their evening exercise (duty), to bed go they likewise, which was in a garret (attic) backward over their master's chamber . . .

The visitor was a rogue. (What do you think happened to the silver on the cupboard once everyone was asleep?) But this part of the story gives us a lot of information. What can you find out from it? For example, how many rooms were there, on how many different floors?

In early Tudor times, even a prosperous townsman would have had simple furniture like this and one room to act as kitchen and living room.

▼

This Tudor drawing of London houses on the bank of the Thames shows how tall and narrow most of them were. Why do you think there are so many sets of steps leading down to the river?

▼

## A CANTERBURY CARPENTER'S
## LIVING ROOM IN 1706

By the end of the Stuart period, even an ordinary craftsman in a small town had different rooms for sleeping and eating, and some luxuries (like the first item in the list below):

|  | £. | s. | d. |
|---|---|---|---|
| In the Lower Room |  |  |  |
| Item one Clocke | 1 |  |  |
| Item one Cubard |  | 4 | 0 |
| Item 3 Tables one forme 5 joint Stools |  | 8 | 0 |
| Item one Kneading Trough & Dresser |  | 2 | 6 |
| Item 6 Chayres |  | 1 | 6 |
| Item one Jacke two Spitts one Dripping pan |  | 3 | 0 |
| Item one payer of Cobirons one Payer of Crepons 2 payers of Tonges & Bellows |  | 3 | 0 |
| Item 7 Pewter Dishes 6 porringers ) 6 Sawsers 14 Spoons 3 Pewter Potts ) 12 pieces of old Pewter ) |  | 14 | 0 |
| Item one Warming pan one pair of ) Cobirons 2 pair of Pot Hooks ) Tosting Irons 2 Skimers One ) Basting Ladle one Case Iron and ) Heters 4 Candelsticks and Candle ) box ) |  | 4 | 0 |
| Item 34 pieces of Earthen wear |  | 3 | 0 |
| Item one fowling piece (gun) |  | 2 | 6 |

What household activity obviously took place in this "Lower Room"? (The clues to this start with Item 6.) What are the most valuable things it contains? When you look at the prices, remember that 8/- (40p) a week was a good wage in 1706. The other rooms listed in this inventory are "the Chamber" (a bedroom), "the Buttery" (used for brewing beer and sometimes as a kind of back-kitchen) and "the Shop".

# Markets

If you look round an old town today, you can usually find the old market area. Sometimes the street names give you a clue. What do you think the London street called "The Haymarket" was used for? Or the street in Oxford called "Cornmarket"?

Why might a fish market be "annoying"? (There is a clue in the last extract on page 21.) What other things were sold in markets, according to Celia Fiennes?

## CELIA FIENNES DESCRIBES TWO MARKETS IN 1698

Large towns had more than one market area. Celia Fiennes took a great interest in the markets of the towns she visited. She has left us some good descriptions.

### Norwich

. . . a broad space called the Haymarket . . . another space for a market to sell hoggs in . . . (one street) is all for stalls for the Country butchers that bring their meate for the supply of the town, which pay . . . a rent for them to the town, on the other side are houses of the Town butchers the Inhabitants, by it is a large market for fish which are all at a little distance from the heart of the Citty so (it) is not annoy'd with them, there is a very large Market place and Hall and Cross for fruite and little things every day, and also a place under pillars for the Corn market . . .

### Exeter

. . . their market day is Fryday which supplies with all things like a fair almost; the markets for meate fowle fish garden things and the dairy produce takes up 3 whole streets, besides the large Market house set on stone pillars which runs a great length on which they lay their packs of serges (cloth).

## OXFORD AND LIVERPOOL MAKE RULES FOR SELLING FISH

Councils spent a lot of time making rules for their markets, and from some of these we can learn who had the right to sell goods and on what day and in which place — as well as what punishments were given for breaking the rules.

◀ *If a town could raise the money, it would build a market hall. This one was built in Faversham in Kent after a Mr Hatch left money for "making a covered market-place . . . paved underneath with broad stones". What was the advantage of having a paved floor?*

*A modern view of the old market-hall, now the Guildhall, in Faversham. The space underneath is still used for the market.*
▼

Whereas it appears . . . that the ancient place of the fishmongers to sell their wett fish on Fridayes, being the Market day for fish, hath been allwayes . . . in certain standings under the Guild Hall and on certain stalls in the streets below . . . . It is att this council agreed that noe fishmonger whatsoever shall after this day sell . . . any wett fish whatsoever, or any fresh salmon (except the said fresh salmon bee first boyled) upon any stall, fish board . . . shopp, or other place, upon the said Friday mornings and untill or after 12 of the clock of the same day in any streete, or open place whatsoever, within this City but in the said fish market . . . . Any one transgressing this act for a day or part of a day is in future to pay a fine of five shillings.
(Oxford Council Acts, March 1659)

Stincking fish: Ed. Voce for bringing unlawfull fish unto market 2/- (fine).
(Liverpool Town Book, 1636)

▲ *A Tudor fish-stall.*

# Schools

Town children had a better chance than country children of receiving at least some education. Most towns had a "petty" school which taught young children to read and write for a small fee. Many Tudor and Stuart towns also had a Grammar School for boys (but not girls) over the age of 8. Rich townsmen sometimes gave their town money to build a school or pay a schoolmaster.

## SCHOOL BUILDINGS

Doctor Edward Jacob, who was born at the end of the Stuart period in Faversham, Kent, described the Grammar School built there in 1582:

> This school-house is very pleasantly situated on the north-side of the churchyard, and consists of a large upper room for teaching the youth, and a smaller for the master, under which is a small room

## FREE SCHOOLING IN OXFORD

A worthy Alderman of this Citty by name Mr. Alderman Nixon . . . hath made the . . . promise of giving Thirty pounds per annum as a yearly stipend for a Schoolmaster to teach thirty or forty Boyes, sones of such of the freemen of this Citty as are not well able to beare the charge of it themselves, to write, read, cast accompt (do arithmetic) . . . and also to have some knowledge of the Latin Tongue so as to fitt them for Apprentices to any Trade whatsoever.
(Oxford Council Acts, April 1658)

Alderman Nixon made the rules for his new school and the Council had his portrait (and his wife's) painted in gratitude. What kind of boys did he intend his school to cater for?

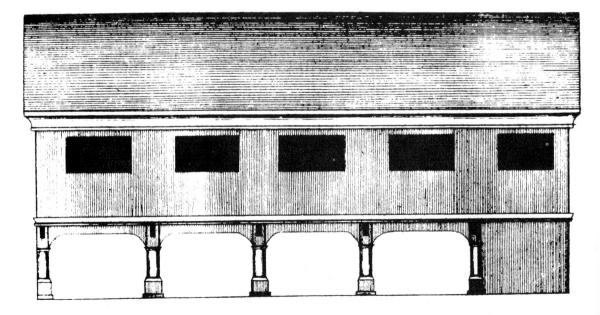

for a library for the use of the school and
a large paved piazza (courtyard or square)
benched, for the diversions of the children,
without being exposed to the weather.
The walk (a gravelled area with 'a fine row
of tall lime trees') also affords a large
scope for their amusements . . .

Faversham School would have pleased the teacher
and text-book writer, Charles Hooke, who gave advice
on school buildings:

The Schoole-house should be a large and
stately building, placed by it self about
the middle of the outside of a Town as
near as may be to the Church, and not far
from the fields, where it may stand in a
good acre, and be free from all annoyances.
It should have a large piece of ground
adjoyning to it, which should be divided
in to a paved court to go round about the
Schoole, a faire Orchard and Garden . . .
and a spacious green close for Scholars
recreations; and to shelter the Scholars
against rainy weather, and that they may
not injure the Schoole in times of play, it
were good if some part of the Court were
sheded, or cloystered over.
 . . . . As for a house of Office (lavatory)
it should be made a good distance from
the schoole, in some corner of the close,
where it may be most out of sight, and
least offensive.
(Charles Hooke, "A New Discovery of the
Old Art of Teaching School", 1660)

A drawing of the Tudor Grammar School at
Faversham. You can see the space left underneath
for the boys to play under cover. The building still
stands today, though it is no longer used as a school.

## ATTENDANCE AT CHURCH

You will see why the school needed to be near the
church from one of the rules for Oundle School in
1566:

That all the Scholars upon the Sabbath
and Holy days resort to the Parish Church
of Oundle in the time of Common Prayer,
the Master or Usher or one of them being
present to oversee them that they do not
misbehave themselves . . .

## DISCIPLINE

School rules also give us a good idea of the behaviour
of Tudor and Stuart boys, and of what kinds of
behaviour older townsmen wanted to encourage and
discourage. Notice the usual punishment for bad
behaviour.

Manchester Grammar School rules, 1528
No scholar . . . (shall) wear any dagger or
other weapon . . . nor bring into the
School, staff (stick) or bat, except their
meat knife.

Oundle School rules, 1566
. . . be it ordered, for every oath or ribald
word spoken in the school or elsewhere,
the Scholar to have three stripes (of the
birch or cane).

Hawkshead School rules, 1585
They shall not haunt taverns, ale houses,
or playing at any unlawful games (such) as
cards, dice . . . or the like.

# Religion

Religious changes affected town-buildings as well as people's lives. In the 1530s Henry VIII broke away from the Roman Catholic church, and had saints' tombs destroyed and monasteries closed. In the Civil War in the 1640s some churches were damaged. After 1689, for the first time, Protestants who disagreed with the Church of England were allowed' to build chapels or meeting-houses. (Roman Catholics still had to worship secretly.)

## CANTERBURY SUFFERS FROM HENRY VIII'S REFORMATION

In 1570 William Lambarde commented on Canterbury which had lost the tourist attraction of St Thomas à Becket's tomb (destroyed in 1538):

> . . . Where wealth is at commandment, how easily are buildings repaired? and

The Orthodox true Minister,

*On Sundays everyone was supposed to go to church. Many people, like John Evelyn, went twice every Sunday and often during the week as well. Townsmen were used to listening to long sermons. They expected to be given good advice by the preacher, and to be scolded for bad behaviour too. John Evelyn described many sermons in his diary:*

> *15 December, 1678*
> *Preach'd Mr Saunders on . . . the reverence due to the house of God: a seasonable discourse there being some in our congregation not so reverent at prayers as they should be.*

*You will notice that the people in the picture are standing. Many churches had no fixed seats. People stood or brought stools to sit on.*

where opinion of great holynesse is, how soone are cities and towns advanced to . . . riches?

And therefore, no marvel, if wealth withdrawn, and opinion of holynesse remooved, the places tumble headlong to ruine and decay.

. . . Canterbury came suddenly from great wealth, multitude of inhabitants, and beautiful buildings, to extreme povertie and decay . . .

Luckily for Canterbury, a group of Protestant immigrants soon arrived from Catholic areas of Europe, escaping from persecution. These immigrants brought valuable skills like silk-weaving and helped to make the town prosperous again.

## THE DESTRUCTION OF MONASTERIES

You might like to find out what happened to any monasteries in the towns near where you live. This is the Tudor historian Leland's account of the new uses found for Malmesbury Abbey:

The whole lodgings of the abbey be now longing to one Stumpe, an exceding rich clothier that bought them of the King . . . . This Stumpe was the chief causer and contributor to have the Abbey Church made a parish church.

At this present tyme every corner of the vast houses of office that belongid to the abbey be full of looms to weave cloth on, and this Stumpe intendeth to make a street or two for clothiers in the back vacant ground of the abbey . . .

## DESTRUCTION IN NORWICH CATHEDRAL IN 1643

Many Parliamentary supporters in the Civil War thought that statues of saints and pictures on walls or in stained-glass were superstitious and wrong. In 1643 the Parliament ordered such objects to be removed. At Norwich this was done very roughly, as Bishop Hall later described:

What clattering of glasses! What beating down of walls! What tearing up of monuments! What pulling down of seats! What wresting out of irons and brass from the windows and graves! . . . What tooting and piping upon the destroyed organ pipes . . .

Later, to the Bishop's horror, the remains of the organ and books for singing the service were burnt in the market place. (The Parliamentarians disapproved of elaborate music in church too.)

## BURY ST EDMUNDS IN THE 1690s

Celia Fiennes was a "Dissenter" (a Protestant who disagreed with the Church of England), and she counted up Dissenters' chapels (meeting places):

. . . there are many Dissenters in the town (Bury), 4 meeting places . . . there is only the ruines of the Abbey walls and the fine gate at the entrance that remains . . .

Notice that Bury has lost one religious building since the beginning of the Tudor period, but gained others. The Church of England churches still remained, of course.

Towns in Tudor and Stuart England were often filthy. Houses had no running water to clean lavatories or make washing easy. Streets and rivers were polluted with all kinds of waste. Germs spread fast and epidemics killed many people. Plague was especially feared.

## MUCK IN THE STREETS AND RIVERS

Animals roaming about the town helped to make the streets dirty.

Maidstone
August 1645
Order touchinge (concerning) Hogges
Whereas the going of Hoggs in the open streetes of this Towne is found by daily experience to be very noisome (smelly) and inconvenient . . . . It is therefore enacted and Ordered . . . that Proclamacion be made by the Cryer of this Towne . . . that noe person or persons . . . shall . . . Permitt or suffer his or theire hogg or hoggs to goe in the High streete, in the Meadow by the Waterside, in Bullock Lane, in Pudding lane, (etc.) . . . upon pain of four pence for every hogg . . .

September 1650
It is Ordered that the Common Cryer of this Towne do make Proclamacion in every streete of this Towne upon

## AN UNHEALTHY TOWN IN CORNWALL

Richard Carew described Tudor Bodmin, with its main street backed by a high hill, so that:

neither can light have entrance to their stairs nor open air to their other rooms. Their back houses, of more necessary than cleanly service, (such) as kitchens, stables etc. are climbed up into by steps, and their filth by every great shower washed down through their houses into the streets . . . their conduit water (the water supply for the town) runneth through the churchyard, the ordinary place of burial for the town. . . . It breedeth therefore little cause of marvel, that every general infection is here first admitted and last excluded . . .

Saturday morning next . . . that no person or persons whatsoever . . . doe presume to sweepe the dirt or dung (at any time henceforward to be upon their . . . pavementes before their . . . houses . . . ) into the Gutter or Gutters of the said streetes whereby the same may be driven into the River . . .
(Maidstone Burghmote Book 4)

Notice how Maidstone Council gets its Orders to the people of the town.

## NOTTINGHAM TRIES TO KEEP THE PLAGUE OUT

The Great Plague in London in 1665 was only the worst of many outbreaks. This extract keeps the original Tudor spelling — see if you can work it out.

Can you see crosses on the doors of the houses with the plague? Stray animals are being killed in case they spread the infection.

1586 December. Order for the Townsfolk to keep away from Derby on account of the Plague there.
No person to go to Derbye neyther to by nor to selle tylle Twelffe Daye be paste nor to go thyther without lycence of Maister Mayre: neyther inkeper nor vytteyler (victualler — seller of food) to receyve anye person of Derbye in to theyre housse in payne of Xs (i.e. on pain of being fined 10/-).

1592-3. We present (accuse) Edmond Garland, of Nottingham, glover, for receiving his sister and keeping her, knowinge that the visitation of God is in the same town where she dwelt.
(Records of Nottingham)

Why do you think the plague was called "the visitation of God"? (You'll find many references in records to "the visited" — meaning plague victims).

## PLAGUE AT DURHAM IN 1597

A town's precautions were often unsuccessful.

Poor Durham this yeare was almost undone. Elvet had the plague first, . . . in John Talentire's house, a walker or lister, and all therein dyed: it began the 14th of May, and few or none escaped it that did not fly into other places. The poorer sort caused Lodges to be made in the moore on this side Durham, and in other places about Durham, but the air being infectious many dyed among them.
(Durham Annals, 1597)

If you would like to find out more about the towns in time of plague, you will find Pepys' Diary very helpful.

# =The Mayor and Aldermen=

It was an honour for a townsman to be chosen (usually by the members of the Town Council) to be a Councillor, and even more of an honour to become an Alderman. Normally, the Aldermen took it in turns to be Mayor for a year: the Mayor had to be elected by all the freemen in most towns, but the freemen usually agreed to choose the Alderman whose turn it was.

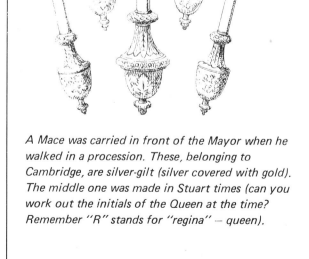

## ALDERMEN IN TUDOR YORK

The Aldermen did not always behave with proper dignity. In 1504 the City of York ordered:

> . . . no alderman of this City from henceforth shall go out of his parish unless that he have a velvet tippet (cape) about his neck and either a man or a child for to attend . . . him in sign and token that he is an alderman . . . for quietness and good order to continue within this city . . . none . . . shall nominate or call any of his brethren Aldermen . . . knave or false knave nor none other . . . name to the rebuke and slander of any of the said persons . . . upon pain to forfeit for every such default . . . 20s.
> **(York Civic Records)**

A Mace was carried in front of the Mayor when he walked in a procession. These, belonging to Cambridge, are silver-gilt (silver covered with gold). The middle one was made in Stuart times (can you work out the initials of the Queen at the time? Remember "R" stands for "regina" — queen).

## A MAYOR'S PROBLEMS

The Mayor during his year of office was a very important man. He represented the King in the town and was responsible for law and order. However, it was all too easy for him to make enemies if he carried out his duties too strictly.

In Stuart Oxford, one Mayor surprised the citizens by not worrying about making himself unpopular:

> Whereas all mayors in the memorie of man use to be mealie-mouthed and fearful of executing their office for feare of losing trade, this person (Robert Pauling, a draper) is not, but walks in the nights to take townsmen in tipling houses (inns) . . . (Anthony à Wood)

The Mayor needed to be a rich man, as you'll see from the following extracts from the Corporation Minutes of Rochester, Kent:

> 5th March 1686
> Whereas John Bryan (Mayor) on behalf of this City has undertaken . . . to buy . . . three tenements (houses) near the High Street and to pull down the same and upon the ground to build . . . a new Guildhall for the City. And Whereas the charges of the said purchase and building up the . . . Guildhall cannot at present be defrayed out of the revenues of the City and must be raised by contributions and free gifts of well-disposed people. It is therefore ordered by the Council that Mr. Mayor and the Aldermen do use their utmost endeavours to gather all such money . . .
>
> 20th September 1707
> Whereas John Bryan . . . had by the desire of the City laid out and expended considerable sums of money in or about the building of the Court Hall (the Guildhall) . . . (and) had expended the sum of £200 more than what had been repaid him by the City, which said sum of £200 the said J. Bryan was prevailed upon and did consent to give . . . the said City, . . . in consideration thereof . . . the said John Bryan should be esteemed and accounted a benefactor of the said City . . .

You can see this new Guildhall in the picture. Why do you think John Bryan was willing to spend his own money on it?

*The Guildhall, Rochester, built in 1684.*

# Elections

By the end of the Stuart period, about 200 towns had the right to elect two Members of Parliament. The people who could vote varied from town to town: in some, it was just members of the council, in others all the freemen. The towns needed MPs who could get things done for them, and so they liked to choose important men, or someone recommended by an important man. The Mayor would try to see that the right candidate was elected. However, if the voters felt strongly, they could and did choose a rival candidate; it was never safe to ignore the ordinary voters.

Cittizens wife

## AN ELECTION CAMPAIGN IN YORK, 1685

Sir John Reresby was Governor of York and a powerful man but, even so, he had a struggle to get elected in 1685. He tells the story of the election in his Diary. First he tried unsuccessfully to persuade the Mayor not to make his rivals freemen (the law said that an MP must be a freeman of the town he represented).

March 10 They having gained this point, I found I was to use all diligence and to spare no charge, if I expected success; and therefore went about the streets from house to house (the Aldermen attending upon me) to ask the

March 13 votes of the citizens, and on the 13th I made a general entertainment throughout the town, viz. in three or four houses in every street, for those to entertain themselves with good liquor that had promised to be for me; though my competitors had begun that custom long before, to gain friends.

March 16 All the candidates went into the streets to gather their party to them, where it was presently seen I had a greater number of followers than any of the rest .... The charge I was at in this election came to £350, though it cost them more that lost it . . .

Reresby got 937 votes, more than anyone else. 1495 people voted.

*Women were not allowed to vote in elections.*

## ELECTION STRUGGLES AT COVENTRY IN 1705

Notice the criticisms which Daniel Defoe makes about unfairness in Coventry elections.

> The City of Coventry . . . sends two Members to Parliament, which are chosen by the Freemen of the City . . . . Things are risen now to that height, that the Parties draw up in little Armies in the Streets, and Fight with all the Fury . . . imaginable, 500, and some say, a 1000 of a side.
>
> . . . And ask any Coventry Man now, who is like to carry it (win the election)? They will Unanimously tell you, They that Beat in the Street, They that get the Victory in the Fight carry the Election, the strongest Side has the Day in the Town Hall. And this may well be true, it seems, since all Freemen Poll (vote) . . . nor is there any lists of the Freemen, so that if the strongest side say a Broom-maker is a Freeman, tho' he never was in the Town, he is Poll'd (his vote is taken) and who shall Dispute against Club-Law?

How do you think the townsmen enjoyed a parliamentary election? Which one of all the methods of gaining votes mentioned in these extracts is still allowed today?

## AN MP AND HIS CONSTITUENCY

However an MP got himself elected, he had to keep on good terms with the townsmen, or he would find himself rejected at the next election. The inscription on Rochester Corn Exchange reads:

> This present building was erected at the sole charge and expense of Sir Cloudesley Shovel, Knight, A.D. 1706. He represented this City in three Parliaments in the reign of King William the Third and in one Parliament in the reign of Queen Anne.

Sir Cloudesley Shovel was an Admiral, and the Navy employed many people in Rochester, so he had a good chance of being favoured at elections. Even so, he kept in close touch with the town.

The bill to Mr. Mayor when Sir Cloudesley Shovel dined

| | |
|---|---|
| Bread and beer | 15. 4 |
| Wine | 9. 11. 8 |
| 6 fowls with beacon and sprouts | 13. 0 |
| A rump of beef | 7. 6 |
| 2 geese with apple sauce | 8. 0 |
| 2 piggs | 8. 0 |
| A Pedgione pye | 8. 0 |
| A Legg of Mutton and Turnipps | 4. 0 |
| A dish of wild fowle | 10. 0 |
| A shoulder of mutton and pickells | 3. 6 |
| A large apple pye and cheese | 4. 0 |
| 2 dishes of mince pyes | 10. 0 |
| Fire | 10. 0 |
| Tobacco | 9. 0 |
| | 15. 2. 0 |

(Rochester City Records, September 1701)

In what ways do you think the Mayor and the MP could be useful to each other?

Large towns, especially London, had a high crime-rate. Visitors from the country were often robbed. John Stow said that a countryman visiting London who had his hood stolen from him in Westminster Hall saw it for sale soon after in Cornhill. He was made to buy it back again. Some thieves stole out of desperation, because they were too poor to buy food. Others, however, made a good living from dishonesty. Stories about daring or unusual crimes were popular, and illustrated broadsheets (single-sheet pamphlets) were sold, giving the gory details.

### THE
## WELCH TRAVELLER;
#### OR THE
## Unfortunate Welchman

#### By HUMPHREY CORNISH

NEWCASTLE.   PRINTED IN THE PRESENT YEAR

*The hero of this story got into all sorts of trouble. As you can see, he spent some time in the stocks, and ended up in the pillory.*

## GETTING MONEY BY FALSE PRETENCES

A famous confidence-trickster in Elizabethan London was called Nicholas Jennings. He told false stories to get sympathy — and money:

> my name is Nicholas Jennings, and I came from Leicester to seek work, and I am a hat-maker by my occupation and all my money is spent; and if I could get money to pay for my lodging this night, I would seek work tomorrow amongst the hatters.

Sometimes he worked with a partner, disguised as a sailor.

> They . . . went abroad to ask charity of the people, feigning (pretending) they had lost their ship with all their goods by casualty on the seas, wherewith they gained much.

Why might Elizabethan Londoners be particularly ready to give money to poor sailors, do you think?

## PLANNED ROBBERIES

Inns were sometimes used as headquarters by robbers. They got information about the guests and later robbed them. The jurymen of Southampton Court Leet in 1576 accused a local inn-keeper of running this kind of inn:

> we present that John Symonds at the White Horse . . . Keepeth resort of lewd (immoral) people both of men and also women . . . of evil name and report and not to be suffered in or about this towne, for . . . a guest called Captain Bartelmew of that house . . . was beset within 3 or 4 myles out of this towne and wayelayde by 5 foot men . . . to be Robbed which guest Reported to his Judgement and thinkinge the watche (on him) to have been made in that house . . .

Some guests turned out to be thieves themselves, as you can see from a story Anthony à Wood tells about an Oxford inn in 1691, where a well-dressed traveller

> called for a room, victualls (food), drinks; the largest plate (silver bowl) in the house to be fill'd with drink, lemons, sugar; silver spoone to mingle it; under pretence of having it stand all night by him in his chamber. In the dead of night he rose, took his horse out of the stable; strew'd straw on the ground that his horse might not be heard; carried away the plate, spoone, pillow, beere, linnen — valued at £15.

You can find another example of an inn keeper being robbed, this time in Canterbury, in the printed collection of extracts from Kent documents called *Kentish Sources: Crime and Punishment.* The Canterbury thieves took the feathers from the feather mattress on the bed!

*Illustrated accounts of crimes were popular with readers.*

# Punishments

Local records show the town authorities punishing townspeople for all kinds of awkward behaviour.

## KEEPING A THIEVING DOG

Sometimes offenders were fined:

... there hath been complaint made of a ... dog between a mastiff and a mongrel of Peter Quotes which ... going lose abroad doth many times offend the neighbours and will fetch out of their houses whole pieces of meat, as loins of mutton and veal and such like and a pasty of venison ... and will not spoil it by the way but carry it whole to his master's house, which being a profitable dog for his master, yet because he is offensive to many it is not sufferable wherefore his master ... (is fined) for every time 3/4d.
(Southampton Court Leet Book)

## HARSH PUNISHMENTS

Many punishments were brutal by today's standards. People were publicly disgraced:

1586, Nottingham
for whippinge of a false boye (a liar) which was sett uppon the pillorie    4d
(Chamberlain's Accounts)

1655, Salford
The Jury doe order that whereas Martha the wife of Peter Farrint did most disorderedly abuse Mr. Adam Warningham then Constable of this towne by most uncivil language ... that the Constables ... shall put the Bridle upon her and (she shall) beare it for one whole houre ...
(Portmote Book)

This was the "scold's bridle", a metal bit put into a woman's mouth.

Now seuen Friends here before haueing beene committed Prisoners Into a nasty stincking Hole in Douer Castle, & there remaineing Prisoners together, namely
1. Thomas Tunbridge,
2. Laurence Knot,
3. Joseph Fuce,
4. Edward Salisbury,
5. Francis Ray,
6. Henery Thrum,
7. Joseph Nicholson.
Shall giue a Relation of some of y exceeding & inhumane Cruelties & wicked Actions (since y King Charles y 2 came into England & landed at Douer) acted (as by many of his Magistrates & Officers of Douer & elsewhere throughout this Nation) soe, Especially, by his Gouernour of Douer Castle Francis Vincent, & his cruel Marshall John Slowman, against an Innocent & Harmlesse People called Quakers Being Prisoners vnder them for y Exercise of a pure Conscience.

◀ Not only criminals were sent to prison. People were imprisoned for their religious views. Here the Quakers (or "Friends" as they called themselves) complain of conditions in Dover Castle in the 1660s.

Savage public punishments, like whipping and execution by hanging, were common. ▶

## GOING TO PRISON

Anyone who was sent to prison had a hard time. Conditions were so bad that many prisoners died from disease. At Maidstone in Kent the gaol was in the middle of the town and even the neighbours complained.

## THE HOUSE OF CORRECTION

Able-bodied beggars were sent to a kind of prison, the House of Correction, where they were made to work, and often whipped as well. Luckily for the prisoners, these places were not always efficiently run. The Mayor of Oxford suggested that alterations were needed there in 1638:

> The Windowes lookinge northward out of the Cellar att the house of Correction are very inconvenient for that such persons as are comitted thither doe not only, instead of workinge, begg out of the same windowes, but also receive instruments into the same whereby they break the barres of the same windowes and soe escape . . .

Look carefully at the picture below and at the handwritten document on page 34 to find out more about punishments at this time. Notice again that most punishments take place in public: what do you think was the reason for this?

1630 — the vaults (cellars) of the gaol begin to be very noisome (smelly), as well to the prisoners . . . as also to the inhabitants of the towne of Maidstone there neare unto adjoining, for want of cleansing and emptying of the same . . .

1638 — some of the inhabitants of Maidstone . . . inhabiting neare unto the gaol there . . . have beene all this winter past and are still much troubled and annoyed with the smoke which commeth out of the said gaole when . . . the prisoners doe make any fyre there, by reason that there is no other means or wayes for the said smoake to issue out but through the windowes of the said gaole . . .

(Extracts from the records of the West Kent Court of Quarter Sessions printed in *Kentish Sources: Crime and Punishment*)

# Disasters

In normal times, the greatest disaster for a town was a big fire. You will probably have heard of the Fire of London in 1666. This was only the worst of many. In 1608, in Bury St Edmunds, 160 houses were burnt. Most of Warwick was destroyed in 1694.

## WAR

The Civil War of 1642-46, between King and Parliament, was a disaster for any town that was attacked by either army. Bolton was taken by the King's troops in 1644 and we have an account written by an indignant supporter of the Parliament.

An Exact Relation of the bloody and barbarous Massacre at Bolton in the Moors in Lancashire, May 28 (1644) . . . being penned by an Eye-Witness . . .
Published according to Order, London . . . August 1644.

. . . when once the horse (the cavalry) was got into the Town there could no resistance almost made, but everyman left to shift for himself . . .
At their entrance, before, behind, to the right, and left, nothing heard but Kill dead, Kill dead was the word in the Town, Killing all before them without any respect, without (outside) the town by their Horsemen pursuing the poore, amazed people, killing, stripping and spoiling (robbing) all they could meet with, nothing regarding the doleful cries of women or children . . . they left almost three score poor widows husband lesse, and hundreds of poor children fatherlesse, and a sweet godly place a nest of owles and a den of dragons, almost without inhabitant . . .

## FIRE IN OXFORD

In 1643 Oxford Council was worried about the state of the fire-fighting equipment for the town. As you will see, they had reason to be anxious.

January 1643
It is agreed that the firehooks of this City made for the pulling down of houses when need shall require in the time of any sudden fire shall be repaired at the City charges; And likewise that two ladders shall be bought by the City to hang ready in the lower hall to be used upon all occasions of fire; And that the chamberlains take care of them and not suffer them to be lent to any person.

By October 1644, the worst had happened:

. . . very many inhabitants whose estates consisted of houses, household stuff, wares and goods are utterly ruined, amongst which 8 common Brewhouses and 10 Bakehouses were burnt . . .

You can find out much more about ways of fighting a fire if you look at Pepys' Diary entries for 1666 (September).

There is a heading over a group of names in the Register of the Parish Church in Bolton: "all these 78 of Bolton slayne the 28 of May 1644". Why is it useful for us to have this extra source of information on the "Bolton Massacre"?

Soldiers behaved badly on both sides, as we can see from a description of a change-over from one side to the other at Nottingham. Lucy Hutchinson, the author, was the wife of Nottingham's Parliamentary governor.

*Fire spread easily along and across narrow streets like this one, with houses built of wood and plaster.*

. . . the Cavaliers that came from Newark, being about six hundred, fell to ransack and plunder all the honest men's houses . . . Their prisoners they . . . put into the sheep pens in the market-place.

(Five days later Parliamentary troops under Sir John Gell arrived.)

As soon as they were come into the town, Sir John Gell's men, seeing the cavaliers had a mind to be gone, interrupted them not, but being as dextrous at plunder as at fight, they presently went to (Alderman) Toplady's house, who had betrayed the town, and plundered it and some others . . .

# Transport

Roads were muddy in winter and dusty in summer. Even town streets were not always paved. Celia Fiennes visited Ely after a rainstorm and wrote that it was "the dirtyest place I ever saw . . . a perfect quagmire the whole citty . . . ".

## TRAFFIC IN THE TOWNS

Town streets were full of horse-drawn carts and people on horseback. Sometimes there were accidents, like Anthony à Wood's in Oxford in 1637 when

> playing before the door of his father's house . . . one of the horses called Mutton belonging to . . . the University carrier, rode over him . . . and bruised his head very much.

By the end of the Stuart period, coach-traffic was increasing. Rich people had their own coaches. Others were able to buy a seat on the public coaches. Coach-services between towns were set up:

> 1669 April 26, Munday, was the first day that the flying-coach went from Oxford to London in one day . . . . They . . . entered into the coach at the tavern door against All Souls College, precisely at 6 of the clock in the morning, and at 7 at night they were all set downe in their inn at London.
> (Anthony à Wood)

Compare this time taken by the "flying-coach" with the time taken by a modern bus or a train to get from Oxford to London today.

## USING THE RIVERS

It was not surprising that people preferred to travel by water if they could. Samuel Pepys often took a boat on the Thames when a Londoner today would take a taxi. Many visitors to London arrived by water. Daniel Defoe wrote about the ferry services from Gravesend:

> it is hardly credible what numbers of people pass here every tide, as well by night as by day, between this town and London. Almost all the people of East Kent, when they go for London, go no farther by land than this town; and then for six-pence in the tilt-boat, or one shilling in a small boat or wherry, are carry'd to London by water.

The rivers were used to carry all kinds of goods too. Defoe described the trade between Reading and London:

> The town lies on the River Kennet but so near the Thames, that the largest barges which they use, may come up to the town bridge, and there they have wharfs to load and unload them. Their chief trade is by this water-navigation to and from London . . . they bring by their barges from London . . . particularly coals, salt, grocery wares, tobacco, oils and all heavy goods.
> They send from hence to London by these barges, . . . very great quantities of timber from Reading . . .

Why would it be sensible to send heavy goods by water and not by road?

*A London coalman's sign showing his cart. Because coal came by sea to London from Newcastle, Londoners called it "sea coal".*

*King's Lynn had a busy trade by river and by sea in this period. This fine Custom House was built in 1683.*

# Growing Towns

Many, though not all, towns grew during this period. London grew enormously, from about 60,000 in 1500 to about 500,000 in 1700. The next largest towns, Bristol and Norwich, grew from about 12,000 to over 20,000, and Birmingham from about 1,000 to about 3,000.

*One of several new towns which grew up in Stuart England was Tunbridge Wells. In this view of 1718, you can see the many visitors who have come to "drink the waters" for their health. (The water was rich in minerals.)* ▶

## MORE HOUSES IN LONDON

John Stow saw open spaces in London becoming built-up areas during his life-time. He wrote in 1598:

> This Hoglane stretcheth north . . . and within these forty years had on both sides fair hedge rows of elm trees, with bridges and easy stiles to pass over into the pleasant fields, very commodious for citizens therein to walk, shoot and otherwise to . . . refresh their dull spirits in sweet and wholesome air, which is now within a few years made a continual building throughout, of garden houses and small cottages . . .

After the Great Fire of 1666, Daniel Defoe noticed how many more houses were being crammed into the empty spaces.

> But tho' by the new buildings after the fire, much ground was given up, and left unbuilt, to enlarge the streets, yet 'tis to be observed, that the old houses stood . . . upon more ground, . . . and in many places, gardens and large yards about them, all which, in the new buildings, are . . . contracted, and the ground generally built up into other houses, so that notwithstanding all the ground given up for beautifying the streets, yet there are many more houses built . . . Swithen's

## BIRMINGHAM OUTGROWS ITS CHURCH

In 1730, William Dugdale described one of the effects of the recent growth of Birmingham's population:

> In the 7th year of Queen Anne, there was an Act of Parliament made, setting forth, that the Town of Birmingham, being a Market Town of great trade and commerce, was becoming very populous, that having but one church in it it could not contain the greater part of the Inhabitants; and that the Churchyard thereof was so little, that the deceased persons could not have decent burial, whereupon it was enacted, that there should be a new Church erected . . .

> Alleys by the Royal Exchange, were all, before the Fire, taken up with one single merchant's house, and inhabited by one Mr. Swithen, whereas upon the same ground where the house stood, stands now about twenty-two or twenty-four houses . . .

How much new building is going on in your local town today?

## NEW FASHIONS IN BUILDING

By the end of the Stuart period, new building meant building in a new style. Celia Fiennes noticed this in Bury St Edmunds when she looked out at the town from a house built in 1693. She saw

> a pleasing prospect of the whole town . . . but no good buildings; except this the rest are great old houses of timber and mostly in the old form of the country which are

> long peaked roofes of tileing; this house is the new mode of building, 4 roomes of a floore, pretty sizeable and high . . .

Look at the pictures of houses in this book (on pages 18-19, 27, 37, for example) and you will find plenty of examples of the "great old houses of timber . . . ". The "new mode of building" was in brick or stone.

# Amusements

Townsmen shared many of the amusements of the country people, like dancing round the Maypole on 1st May and playing foot-ball with a blown-up pig's bladder. In London, going to the theatre was popular by late Tudor times. Shakespeare's plays were performed in the open-air Globe. Stuart theatres were roofed-over and more expensive.

## MAIDSTONE TOWN COUNCIL BANS ROUGH SPORTS IN 1653

Some pastimes were so brutal that people began to turn against them in the Stuart period. Even games of football (which took place in the streets) could get dangerously rough.

> Whereas . . . it hath beene seene that many inconveniences have arisen by means of people congregating themselves together in a rude and unlawfull manner in the streetes and other open places of this Towne upon days commonly called Shrove Tuesdays and other days Playinge at football and cudgells (fighting with long sticks), tossing of dogs and . . . throwing at cockes and other poultry in a cruel unchristianlike manner, For the prevention whereof for the future It is Ordered that whatsoever person shall . . . produce or bringe forth any cudgells or football to be sported with . . . shall forfeit . . . Two shillings and sixpence for every time And that whatsoever person shall there play at the said sports called cudgells or football shall for every such time forfeit . . . twelve pence.
> (Maidstone Burghmote Book)

(The penalty for bringing animals or poultry to be thrown at was also set at twelve pence.)

*Dancing round a maypole in the time of Charles I. What kind of music is being provided for the dance?*

## BEAR-BAITING AND COCK-FIGHTING

John Stow described the arrangements for bear-baiting in Southwark in the 1590s:

> there be two bear gardens, the old and new places, wherein be kept bears, bulls and other beasts, to be baited; as also mastiffs in several kennels, nourished to bait them. These bears and other beasts are there baited in plots of ground, scaffolded about for the beholders to stand safe.

In 1663, Samuel Pepys went to a cock-fight:

> 21 December   To Shoe Lane to see a cock-fighting at a new pit there, a sport I was never at in my life: but Lord, to see the strange variety of peoples, from Parliament-man (an MP) . . . to the poorest 'prentices, bakers, brewers, butchers, draymen, and what not: and all these fellows one with another cursing and betting. I soon had enough of it.

## PEPYS AT THE THEATRE

Pepys preferred plays to cock-fights:

> 1661 3 January.   To the Theatre, where was acted 'Beggars Bush', it being very well done; and here the first time that ever I saw women come upon the stage.

Do you know who played the women's parts in plays before the 1660s?

## CELEBRATIONS

On big occasions the townsmen enjoyed celebrating in the streets. In 1660, after years of war and upheaval, Oxford Council spared no expense on the day the new King Charles II was proclaimed. They arranged:

> that a Hogshead of Claret (wine) bee . . . put into the Conduit and running in Two pipes Eastwards and Southward, that there be 80 dozen of Cakes . . . att and about the conduit, that there be such Trumpets provided as Mr. Mayor . . . shall thinke fit . . . that there bee 10 Barrells of double Beere for the entertainment of the Commons (people) and of the Soldiers this day, that there bee 100 dozone of Bread for the poor . . .

*Making music was a popular pastime. This sign belonged to a maker of musical instruments in the 1690s. His shop was near St Paul's Cathedral in London.*

# Difficult Words

| | |
|---|---|
| *Alderman* | a senior member of a town council. |
| *chandler* | a maker or seller of candles, often a grocer as well. |
| *city* | a large town, with a cathedral. |
| *cobirons* | used to hold up the spit (see below). |
| *conduit* | a water-pipe. |
| *cony, cony-catching* | a cony was a rabbit: the term was also used for someone who was easily deceived — so "cony-catching" meant going round tricking people. |
| *cordwainer* | a leatherworker or shoemaker. |
| *currier* | a leatherworker. |
| *gittern* | a musical instrument like a guitar. |
| *guild* | a company of merchants or craftsmen. |
| *Guildhall* | a place where members of a guild met: sometimes used by a town council so the word is also used for a town hall. |
| *hose, jagged* | breeches slashed to show another material underneath. |
| *hosen* | stockings. |
| *jack* | used for turning a spit (see below) over a fire. |
| *joint-stool* | a small wooden stool. |
| *kneading-trough* | a trough for making dough to make bread. |
| *maltster* | a man who makes malt (used in beer-brewing). |
| *peer* | a nobleman. |
| *porringer* | a small bowl. |
| *poverty-line* | to live "on the poverty-line" means to be constantly in danger of hunger and cold. |
| *Quaker* | a member of the Society of Friends, a religious group founded in the 1650s. |
| *spit* | a pointed metal rod on which meat was put to roast over a fire. |
| *tilt-boat* | a large rowing-boat with an awning to shade the passengers. |
| *usher* | an assistant school-master. |
| *warming-pan* | a metal pan rather like a covered frying pan. Hot coals were put inside and the pan was put in the bed to warm it. |
| *wherry* | a rowing-boat. |

## CONVERSION TABLE

| NEW MONEY | | OLD MONEY |
|---|---|---|
| 1p | = | 2.4d |
| 5p | = | 1s. (1 shilling) |
| 50p | = | 10s. (10 shillings) |
| £1 | = | £1 |
| | | 12d = 1 shilling |
| | | 20 shillings = £1 |

# Biographical Notes

## TUDOR AND STUART KINGS AND QUEENS

### The Tudors

| | |
|---|---|
| 1485-1509 | Henry VII |
| 1509-1547 | Henry VIII |
| 1547-1553 | Edward VI |
| 1553-1558 | Mary I |
| 1558-1603 | Elizabeth I |

### The Stuarts

| | |
|---|---|
| 1603-1625 | James I (James VI of Scotland, where he had been King since 1567) |
| 1625-1649 | Charles I (1649-1660 England had no King: 1653-1658 Oliver Cromwell was Lord Protector) |
| 1660-1685 | Charles II |
| 1685-1688 | James II |
| 1689-1694 | William III and Mary II (Mary died 1694) |
| 1694-1702 | William III |
| 1702-1714 | Anne |

AUBREY, John (1626-1697) wrote *Brief Lives*, short biographies of many Stuart people.

CAREW, Richard (1555-1620) wrote a local history, *The Survey of Cornwall*.

DEFOE, Daniel (about 1661-1731) worked as a journalist. He also wrote *Robinson Crusoe*, and a travel book, *A Tour Through Great Britain*.

EVELYN, John (1620-1706) wrote a famous diary.

FIENNES, Celia (1662-1741) wrote *The Journal of Celia Fiennes*, describing her travels in Britain. Her *Journal* was not published until the nineteenth century.

HUTCHINSON, Lucy (1620-date of death unknown, but sometime after 1675) wrote a biography of her husband, *Memoirs of the Life of Colonel Hutchinson*. He fought for Parliament against the King in the Civil War.

LAMBARDE, William (1536-1601) wrote a local history, *Perambulation of Kent*, as well as several books about English laws and law-courts.

LELAND, John (about 1506-1552) was a scholar who travelled round England and Wales. His notes were made into a book, *The Itinerary of John Leland*.

PEPYS, Samuel (1633-1703) kept a very detailed diary of his life in London from 1660 to 1669. He worked for the Navy as a civil servant.

STOW, John (about 1525-1605) wrote a history and description of London called *Survey of London*. It was published in 1598.

WOOD, Anthony à (1632-1695) lived in Oxford and wrote about the town and the University. He also kept a diary.

# Book List

## Records in print

The records of many towns have been published in whole or in part, including those of Leicester, Maidstone, Newcastle, Nottingham, Oxford, Salford, Southampton, York. Detailed modern histories of towns also often include short extracts from town records.

N.B. Your *county archives* may publish pamphlets or kits, like the Kent series, *Kentish Sources*, or the Essex selection of photostats and other material, *Essex Towns*.

## Books for younger readers

Batsford's *Growing Up* series, especially *Growing up in Tudor Times* and *Growing up in Stuart Times*.

Longman's *Then and There* series, especially *The Elizabethan Citizen*, and *Samuel Pepys in London*.

## Books for older readers

Ashley, Maurice, *Life in Stuart England*, Batsford 1967

Clark P. and Slack P., *English Towns in Transition, 1500-1700*, Oxford University Press, 1976

Hoskins, W.G., *Provincial England*, Macmillan, 1963

Judges, A.V. (editor), *The Elizabethan Underworld*, Routledge, 1930

McInnes, Angus, *The English Town, 1660-1760*, Historical Association, 1980

Williams, Penry, *Life in Tudor England*, Batsford, 1964

# Places to Visit

The towns themselves: the photographs in this book suggest some of the places to go to see Tudor and Stuart buildings. Some towns use Tudor or Stuart houses as museums, or just open them to the public. Part of Maidstone Museum is a Tudor house. Stranger's Hall Museum in Norwich is in a pre-Tudor house extended by Tudor and Stuart merchants. Rowley's House in Shrewsbury was the home of a Tudor merchant and Shrewsbury's Public Library is kept in the old Tudor grammar school building. In Salisbury, Mompesson House is a good example of a late Stuart house in the "new style" of building. York has old streets like Pavement and The Shambles, and (like many towns) the ruins of a monastery destroyed by Henry VIII. Berwick-on-Tweed has Tudor walls and a church built just after the Civil War. Ipswich has a late Stuart "meeting house" — the present Unitarian Church. At Newark, which was besieged in the Civil War, you can see the remains of old fortifications used in the siege, and weapons of the time in the town museum.

The London Museum, Barbican, London (very good sections on Tudor and Stuart London)

The Geffrye Museum, Kingsland Road, Shoreditch, London (shows what Tudor and Stuart living rooms were like, and has excellent teaching sessions on town life in the past).

*The map shows important battles in the Civil War, as well as towns. Battles are marked* ⚔.

SCOTLAND

Berwick on Tweed

NORTH SEA

Newburn • Newcastle

Durham

Lancaster • Scarborough

Preston • York
Bradford • Marston Moor
Bolton • Leeds • Selby
Salford • Hull
Liverpool
Sheffield

Gainsborough

Newark • Lincoln

Derby • Nottingham

Shrewsbury

Birmingham • Leicester

King's Lynn • Norwich

Coventry • Naseby

Pembroke

Worcester • Edge Hill
Cropredy Bridge • Cambridge • Bury St Edmunds

Gloucester • Oxford • Ipswich

Cardiff • Colchester

Bristol • Brentford • London

Newbury • Reading
Taunton • Bridgwater • Rochester
Langport • Salisbury • Maidstone
Exeter • Alresford • Canterbury
Bodmin • Southampton • Portsmouth • Tunbridge Wells • Dover
Lostwithiel
Plymouth

IRISH SEA

0          100
          Km

ENGLISH CHANNEL

47

# Index